UNICORN CRAFTS

MORE THAN 25 MAGICAL PROJECTS TO INSPIRE YOUR IMAGINATION

ISABEL URBINA GALLEGO

Racehorse Publishing

Racehorse Publishing books may be purchased in bulk at special discounts for sales promotion, corporate gifts, fund-raising, or educational purposes. Special editions can also be created to specifications. For details, contact the Special Sales Department, Skyhorse Publishing, 307 West 36th Street, 11th Floor, New York, NY 10018 or info@skyhorsepublishing.com.

Racehorse Publishing™ is a pending trademark of Skyhorse Publishing, Inc.®, a Delaware corporation.

Visit our website at www.skyhorsepublishing.com.

10 9 8 7 6 5 4 3 2 1

Library of Congress Cataloging-in-Publication Data is available on file.

Cover design by Michael Short
Cover photography by Isabel Urbina Gallego

ISBN: 978-1-63158-303-2
E-Book ISBN: 978-1-63158-304-9

Printed in Canada

CONTENTS

SAFETY INFORMATION

- It is recommended that all crafts and activities in this book be supervised by an adult.

- Always take safety precautions when undertaking manual tasks and activities. Always follow the labels of the ingredients and supplies used.

- Always use your best judgment and do not allow children under the age of three to handle ingredients or small supplies that may be a choking hazard.

- Adults should handle any chemical products or sharp tools.

INTRODUCTION

If this book has reached your hands, surely it's because, like me, you love crafts and unicorns.

Hello, everyone! My name is Isa, and I have created this book with a lot of love especially for you. However, before you start, let me tell you a little more about me.

I have always liked making crafts, but it was three years ago when I decided to share my hobby with the world through my YouTube channels Isa's World (in English) and El Mundo de Isa (in Spanish), where I upload videos every week with tutorials explaining how to make crafts of all styles: kawaii, vintage, Tumblr, country, etc. I also create DIY tutorials for room decorating, organizing supplies, crafts for school, and more!

If you haven't heard of or visited my channels, I would be very happy if you visited, especially if you become part of my virtual club with which I love to share this hobby.

Throughout this book, you'll notice I have incorporated hashtags so you can showcase your finished projects! When you replicate one of the handicrafts in this book, upload a photo to any social network with the "#IsasUnicornCrafts" hashtag, so I can see it and give you a like, 😍, or comment.

In this book you will discover twenty-seven fun crafts inspired by unicorns, explained step by step, that will awaken your most magical and creative side.

You can use the crafts you create to customize a party, organize your school supplies, or give as gifts, among many other practical uses.

I hope you enjoy this book as much as I have enjoyed writing it and that through its pages the spirits of unicorns fill your heart with a rainbow of happiness.

Be a unicorn. Let's get started!

If you don't have a green thumb, it's better to have plants that don't need much watering.

Unicorn Cactus Pot

I love growing plants, but if I'm being honest, even my cactuses dry up. I'm not sure what I'm doing wrong, but for some reason I'm not the best gardener.

I thought that I'd never be able to have a plant on my table, but I didn't let my doubts get the best of me. I needed a solution to my problem, so I thought to myself: *Stones can't dry up!*

I set out on a Sunday morning to create this project, and at the end of the afternoon I had a beautiful unicorn pot on my desk. The difficulty for this project is medium.

Supplies:

- Clay pot
- Acrylic paints (colors: white, light green, and dark green)
- Pink and green Model Magic
- Golden foam paper with glitter
- Super glue
- Black permanent marker
- Soft brush
- Pink chalk
- 4 elongated stones
- 2 small artificial flowers

Instructions:

I have chosen a 6-inch (diameter) ceramic pot for this project, but this craft does not require exact measurements, so you can choose any size pot that you like.

First, paint the pot with white acrylic paint; for better coverage apply two coats of paint, allowing the pot to dry between layers. Let it dry completely. Meanwhile, you can move on to the next step.

Decorate the top rim with some roses. To make the roses, use pink and green Model Magic. Make a bunch of pink balls, about the size of a pea, and crush each with the tip of your finger.

Roll the dough with your finger, as shown in the following image. We will call this shape the heart of the rose. Each rose needs a single heart, so make as many as roses as you'd like or fill up the pot's rim entirely.

Shape the remaining balls to form drops, then squash them to form the petals. Each rose needs at least fifteen petals. Make sure the petals are different sizes; you'll place the smaller ones in the center of the rim and the larger ones on the outside.

Begin to form the rose. At this point in the process, surely the petals are almost dry and do not stick together, so it will be necessary to apply a little water with a brush that will act as glue.

Place the petals one by one to form the rose. You can use as many petals as you want; my roses have between twelve and sixteen petals each. To give a touch of green color, place four or five elongated leaves on the last petal layer.

Once the white paint on the pot is dry, continue decorating it. The horn of the unicorn is created by cutting a triangle of gold foam paper with glitter. Depending on the size of your pot and the gold paper foam, the horn should have a height of approximately 3 ¼ inch. Paste the horn to the pot with a glue that sticks to ceramic. Super glue works well. Then paste five roses that will decorate the front of the unicorn, using the same glue.

With a black permanent marker, draw the unicorn's eyes. To make your pot's eyes look like mine, they should each have two curved lines with five eyelashes each. Also add some rosy blush on the pot's face. I used pink chalk and applied it with a soft brush.

Great, now you have a beautiful pot! If you'd like, you can stop here and place a beautiful plant inside. However, if you want an immortal cactus, keep working. It's very close to being finished!

Look for a few elongated stones that have a smooth surface. Paint them with different shades of green and add a few touches of white to simulate the thorns of a cactus. You can paint polka dots, stripes, or crosses so that they look almost like real plants!

Finally, decorate the cactus with some artificial fabric flowers. Stick them on the cactus using the same glue from previous steps. To position the cactus inside the pot, fill it with decorative white sand, which you can buy at any plant store.

If you like to give away things you created with your own hands, this craft is a perfect gift!

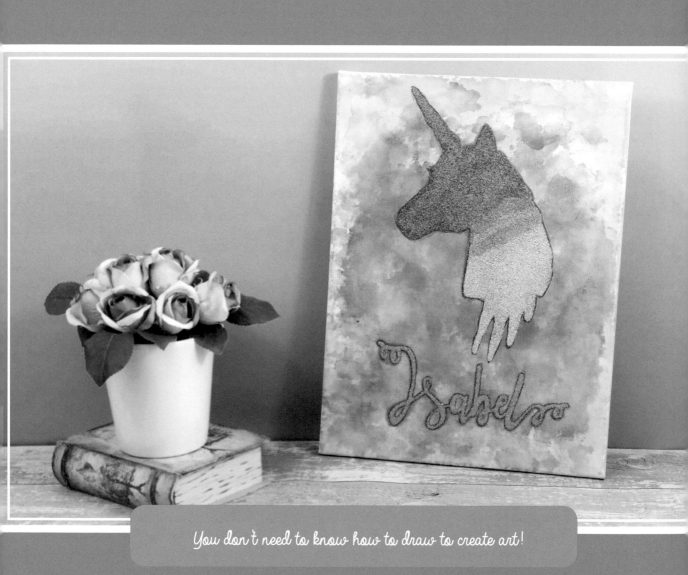

You don't need to know how to draw to create art!

Unicorn Watercolor Canvas

I have always liked canvases painted with watercolors, especially those with tons of colors! What I like most is the combination of blue, pink, and lilac colors that are so characteristic of unicorns. Recently, I learned an easy trick to create this effect and I'm going to share it with you. It's so easy that you won't even need watercolors.

This project has a low level of difficulty and does not require much work. It will take you less than one hour plus drying time.

Supplies:

- White canvas
- Acetate sheet (or similar type of plastic)
- Paper towels
- Markers (not permanent) in blue and pink colors
- Water
- Sheet of paper
- Pencil
- Fine brush
- White glue
- Blue and silver glitter

Instructions:

As I mentioned previously, I'm going to show you a trick to paint watercolor backgrounds using markers. You will need a sheet of acetate (or similar plastic) and paper towels to clean the plastic after each use.

Using the markers, add color to different areas along all the plastic. Do not mix the colors and leave a little separation between the spots.

Put drops of water on the canvas. Note: Do not put the drops close together. In the following image, you can see that I am applying the drops of water with a dropper that allows them to come out one

by one. However, if you don't have a dropper, don't worry—you can do it with your finger! Just dip the tip of your finger in a glass of water and when you remove it, a drop will remain. Then place the drop on the canvas.

Now take the plastic and place it on the canvas so the drops of water and marker ink come into contact with one another. Keep the plastic on the canvas for a few seconds so that the colored water spots spread out and the canvas absorbs the colors. Then clean the plastic with a paper towel and repeat this process as many times as you want until the entire canvas is full of color.

On a sheet of paper, draw a unicorn silhouette. If you aren't good at drawing, you can find a silhouette on the Internet and print it out. Then cut it out to use it as a template. Place the silhouette on the canvas and trace its outline with a pencil.

Next, fill in the silhouette that you just drew with white glue. Use a fine brush to avoid getting glue outside of the pencil lines. If some glue spills off the silhouette and onto the canvas, take some cloth and clean it. It is important that only the inside of the silhouette has glue.

Isn't this technique easy?

Sprinkle glitter on the glue. For my unicorn, I decided to put blue glitter on the top and silver on the bottom, but you can use whatever colors you like! Pour the excess glitter onto a paper and save it to use in another project. You will notice that the glitter has stuck to the glue and now the whole silhouette is filled with glitter. Do you love it as much as I do?

This canvas can be a great gift for someone special. You can customize it with that person's name. I put my own name because I'm giving it to myself! Repeat the same process as you did with the glitter on the silhouette, only now on the letters of the name. Then let the whole piece dry for two hours.

Finally, put some white glue on the silhouette and name, covering all areas of glitter. This must be done to protect it, so that the glitter does not detach over time. Don't worry if everything looks white; when it dries, the glue will become transparent.

I'm in love with this technique. This unicorn canvas looks like a true work of art. 😊

A special place to put your important photos and notes!

Unicorn Cork Board

#UnicornBoard #INeedToTakeNotesForImportantThings
#SpiritOfAUnicornButTheMemoryOfAFish #IsasUnicornCrafts

I'm *sooo* excited about this project, guys! I needed a place to put my important notes and I was about to buy a cork board, but they were all so boring. Most were just square boards with a brown wooden frame . . . definitely not for me! I needed something fun and beautiful, so I thought: *Do it yourself!*

This is one of the easiest crafts you'll find in this book, and it takes very little time to complete. You can likely finish it in less than an hour.

Supplies:

- Pencil
- Cork sheet (¼ inch thick)
- Scissors
- Cardboard (¼ inch thick)
- White glue
- Fine-tipped paint brush
- Acrylic paints (pink and white colors)
- Soft brush
- Foam paper glue
- Pink foam paper
- Double-sided tape to stick on the wall

Instructions:

Draw with pencil on the cork a simple outline of a unicorn's profile. I have only drawn the head. It is not necessary to draw details, just the outline will suffice.

Cut out the unicorn's profile using the outside contour as a guide. Cork is a soft material that is easily cut, but do it slowly and carefully. You don't want to crack it!

Use this figure as a template and trace the outline on cardboard. This cardboard must be at least ¼ inch thick, which will give you the necessary depth for adding your pins and pushpins.

Cut out the shape on the cardboard, then glue the cardboard and corkboard together using white glue. Make sure that both figures are centered and then place it on a flat surface to dry. The cardboard absorbs moisture from the glue, so it is necessary to place a few heavy books on top of the project while it dries. If no weight is placed on top, it may bend and warp the design.

Once the glue is dry, it's time to paint! Choose whichever color acrylic paints you like. For my corkboard, I painted the unicorn's hair pink and used white on the horn. I decided not to paint the face because I like the contrast between the colors and the cork.

When I create beautiful crafts with my own hands, I feel indescribable satisfaction!

To finish the project, you can paste a super thin strip of foam paper around the perimeter of the unicorn to give it a more professional look. Use a glue that is appropriate for gluing foam paper.

If you want to stick your cork board on the wall, you can use special double-sided tape.

Customize your cup and everyone will want one like yours!

Unicorn Cup

#UnicornCup #ThisCupIsOnlyMine #IsasUnicornCrafts

In my family, I'm known as the "cup-giver." They are my weakness. I love having tea in the middle of the afternoon, but I think it tastes better if you drink it in a nice cup. I have tons of mugs and cups, but I was missing a decorated one with an adorable unicorn. This DIY project is easy, but you need the help of an adult because you have to use the oven. It will take approximately three hours to complete.

Supplies:

- Polymer clay (colors: magenta, white, yellow, beige, blue, and purple)
- Porcelain cup
- Super glue (or a glue that sticks to porcelain)
- Modeling clay tools
- Oven

Instructions:

This time we will use polymer clay. It is a modeling clay that needs to be dried in an oven. Despite this extra step, the result is incredible. We will use this clay because the finished product can then be washed without being damaged, so it is perfect for decorating a cup.

First, get a porcelain cup with a smooth surface. Mine will have a unicorn seated on a cupcake.

Next, start modeling the base of the cupcake. The polymer clay is a little hard when you first open the package; therefore, you will need to knead it for several minutes until it softens and becomes easier to shape.

Take a piece of magenta clay and make a shape like the one you can see in the following image using the modeling tools. This will be the cupcake liner. Position it in its appropriate place on the cup and press a little so that it stays stuck.

To make the sponge part of the cake, use a piece of beige dough, make an oval shape (but somewhat irregular), and position it in its appropriate place. Remember to softly press the clay on the cup so that it sticks.

Make some details to make it look like a real cupcake: using different colors of clay, add a little white cream on top, some sprinkles, and some polka dots on the cupcake liner. Also, make a few lines in the liner to make it more realistic.

The picture shows you the white clay shapes that you will need to make the unicorn. In the upper part of the image, you can see the head and the ears. In the lower part, you can see the body, the front legs, and the hind legs. These are very easy to make.

Place each piece on the cup to form the unicorn. Add a pair of light pink circles on the hind legs and a beige oval shape that serves as the unicorn's snout.

In the next image, you can see some of the details that are shaping this little unicorn. Starting from the top, I have added some small light pink circles to the ears, a small yellow drop that serves as the horn, and an assortment of small colorful clay strands to create the mane. Two small black balls are the unicorn's eyes and two light pink balls can be used as the blush. I used the back of a paintbrush to make the holes for the nostrils. If you keep looking, you'll also notice that I have made a tail using various colors of clay.

You can complete your design with a few colored circles and some candy clouds made with lilac, pink, and white clay. When you have finished decorating the cup, it will be time to bake it. Look at the clay's instructions for the temperature and time that the manufacturer recommends. In my case, it indicates thirty minutes at 230°F.

When the baking time is over, let the cup cool down. The clay pieces should have hardened with the shape of the cup. These should be easy to remove.

This is a super kawaii cup. I love it!

Once you have removed the clay pieces, clean the cup with a dry cloth and apply glue to the back of each piece of clay, then stick them on the cup in their proper places. I used an instant glue that sticks on porcelain. Once it has dried, the cup will be ready to use.

Tip: This cup should not be put in the microwave or in the dishwasher; always handwash with cold water and rub lightly with a soft sponge.

A frappuccino with everything, please!

Kawaii Unicorn Frappuccino Handbag

#Unicornfrappuccino #KawaiiHandbag
#UnicornHandbag #IsasUnicornCrafts

Here's how it typically goes when I enter a café:

Me: "Hello! A frappuccino, please."

Barista: "Do you want any toppings?"

Me: "Sure, put a lot of cream, caramel-flavored syrup, nuts, marshmallows, colored chips, chocolate chips, a little bit of that edible unicorn glitter. Ah! And one of those decorative umbrellas."

Barista: "Are you sure? I think there will hardly be room for your frappuccino."

Me: "It doesn't matter, I'd prefer the sweets 😄!"

I love those coffee shops where they have all kinds of sweet drinks. I was inspired by the Unicorn Frappuccino to make this very original handbag. This craft's difficulty level is medium, and it can be completed in approximately three hours.

Supplies:

- Baking sheets
- Pencil
- Foam paper (colors: white, black, fuchsia, blue, light pink, turquoise, and three small pieces of yellow, red, and lilac)
- Liquid silicone glue (or super glue)
- Blue and pink glitter
- Scissors
- Pink, blue, and turquoise markers
- Cotton swabs
- White acrylic paint
- Cord or ribbon to hang the bag

Instructions:

I have designed this animated unicorn frappuccino bag to be in style of kawaii. It's so adorable with its rosy cheeks!

I must warn you that we will use foam paper for this project. Therefore, you will not be able to put much weight in your bag, but you can use it to play or carry things that are not too heavy.

With this project, I will teach you a trick to transfer any drawing to foam paper. You will need baking sheets; this is a vegetable paper that has a thin wax film on its surface, which makes it ideal for our purposes.

Trace the design with a pencil on the baking sheet. You can do it all at once or trace each colored piece separately. In my case, I have decided to trace the outer contour on one sheet, and the icing and the details of the cup on another. I think that it's easier this way to transfer the templates to their corresponding colors of foam paper.

Then turn the baking sheet over on the foam paper, place each template on top its corresponding color (so that the graphite from the pencil is touching the foam paper).

Now hold the paper with one hand, keeping it steady. Use something rounded on the lines of the templates to transfer the pencil's graphite to the foam paper. I used the handle of the scissors.

When you remove the paper, you will notice that the template has been printed on the foam paper. Now, cut out each piece with the scissors.

Tip: Foam paper is a very easy material to cut. However, to make sure that the edges are uniform requires some practice and technique. When cutting foam paper, try to make the cuts of the scissors long and clean. Instead of moving the scissors while cutting, it is better to move the foam paper in curved sections and keep the scissors in the same position.

Next, begin to form the front of the bag. As you can see in the following image, I cut a piece of black foam paper that is the total contour of the drawing. This piece is where you will glue all the others. But before doing this, I will teach you how to shade the colored pieces; this will add depth to the final product.

Use markers (not permanent) with colors similar to the pieces of foam paper that you have to shade, except for the white foam paper where we will use blue and pink shading. Color the entire edge of the foam paper with a line using a marker and then blend it with a cotton swab. You must shade all the pieces. The shading can be underwhelming and may not seem necessary, but when the whole design is formed, it will give the creation depth and a more realistic look.

Next, paste each piece on the black background using liquid silicone glue or super glue. In this case, I have used super glue because it dries instantly.

Decorate the cream area with pink and blue glitter. Put glue on the areas you want to decorate and then sprinkle the glitter. Shake off the excess and let it dry. With white acrylic paint, paint a couple of light points inside each eye.

It has a kawaii face—so adorable!

To make the back of the bag more resistant, I cut another black outline of the frappuccino and I glued it to the other black outline with super glue to double up. In this step, you must be precise so that both pieces match perfectly.

To make the bag, cut two foam paper pieces that are 2 ¾ inches wide and 15 ¾ inches long. Join them together with glue, but leave a gap in the center of both ends where we will put the cord/string to hang it.

Glue this strip through the lower edge of the bag, leaving a margin of approximately ½ inch. Then stick this to the front of the bag. Be precise when placing the back piece to match the front.

Finally, cut a cord strip long enough to hang the bag from your shoulder and stick it inside the hole you left unglued. Use enough glue to make it very strong and let it dry by pressing with your fingers.

Ready! I think that today I will wear my new bag when I go to my favorite cafe.

Unicorn Galaxy Shoes

#UnicornShoes #UnicornFashion #UnicornStyle
#ILiveInAUniverseOfUnicorns #IsasUnicornCrafts

I think unicorns come from a distant galaxy—a galaxy full of pink, blue, and lilac colors, and surely everything is full of glitter. For this project, we will create a unicorn galaxy on our shoes. Be prepared to be looked at and asked a thousand times where you bought these cool kicks.

It's a quick craft to do. It takes approximately two hours plus drying time, and it's also extremely easy. Ready?

Supplies:

- White cloth sneakers
- Masking tape
- Blue, pink, and white textile paint
- 3 disposable plastic cups
- 2 teaspoons
- Paint sponge
- Toothbrush
- Brush
- Water

Instructions:

You can recycle used white shoes or buy new ones to personalize them.

Whatever your choice, first remove the laces and cover the soles with masking tape. Make sure to cover them completely, since any gap can stain them permanently. So, take your time to cover the entire sole and the toe cap, as seen in the image below.

The paints need to have a liquid texture so that it's easier to mix the colors. Put a teaspoon of blue paint in a plastic cup, add a little water, and stir until you get a thinner texture (be sure not to make it too watery). Do the same with the pink paint.

With a painting sponge, apply both mixtures you just made to the shoes. Try to combine the colors, but do not mix too much. Clean the sponge with clean water every time you change color. The goal is to create pink areas and blue areas. Subsequently, lilac areas will appear where both colors mix.

Amazing! Let's begin to paint our galaxy!

And what is a galaxy without stars? We will create beautiful stars and sparkles with white paint. Scatter small white dots across the backdrop with a fine-tipped paint brush.

To create shooting stars, use a toothbrush (the brush you use should no longer be used to brush your teeth; use an old brush for this craft and then keep it with your supplies for other projects). Put white paint on the bristles of the brush and sprinkle the shoes by running your finger over the bristles; you will get splashes similar to the trails of shooting stars. Repeat this a few times for each shoe.

With a fine-tipped brush and white paint, draw crosses and full stars. These will be the brightest stars in the galaxy

You are doing super well! Let the shoes dry, and meanwhile, we will continue customizing the laces.

Place the laces inside a plastic cup and pour in a mixture of pink paint and water until the cords are covered completely. Then, with the help of your brush handle, swish around the cords so that they absorb all the liquid and are soaked with pink!

Leave them in the cup for thirty minutes, then spread the laces and shoes out on a plastic sheet. Let them dry outdoors. It will take a whole day to dry, so be patient and do not use them until they have dried completely.

If your shoes are already dry, it's time to remove the masking tape. Note that all the areas you covered with the tape are clean and the shoes look new.

Use a damp cloth to clean the holes where the laces should be woven, as they are traditionally made of metal and can be easily cleaned.

Finally, weave the laces once they have dried completely. Now you can use your brand new unicorn galaxy shoes! Don't you love them? This craft is a perfect gift for a friend who loves unicorns; just find out their shoe size, and you can make a unique and perfect present.

I'm afraid I have some new favorite shoes, and I'm thinking that maybe I can create more galaxy-style unicorn apparel with the same technique. 🤔

Personalize your headphones, so they are entirely unique!

Unicorn Headphones

I use my headphones daily, but I think they look *soooo* boring. Personalizing your headphones is easy and fast; it only takes approximately one hour to do so. However, this type of modeling compound is slow drying, so you will have to wait twenty-four hours to be able to use them.

Supplies:

- Headphones
- Model Magic (colors: white, pink, blue, yellow, and black)
- Super glue
- Toothpick or tool for clay that has a fine tip

Instructions:

I love Model Magic. It is light, easy to work with, air dries, and the pieces stick to each other on contact. We will use this clay to personalize your headphones, so they will look stylish. It will appear as if little unicorns are poking their heads out of your ears! It's cute and fun!

Considering that we are dealing with a pair of headphones, you must make two unicorn heads—one for each ear. My advice is to make them simultaneously. By doing this, it will be easier to keep them consistent, so do everything I explain in the following text twice.

Whenever I use a modeling compound, I start by making a ball or sphere. From this, I make all the other shapes that I need. Take a small amount of Model Magic and roll it into a ball, then mold to get a drop shape (as seen in the image). The drop should measure about one inch. This will be the head of the unicorn.

Next, you will need a small gray ball. To get this color, you must mix black and white. Use approximately one tenth of black in proportion to white to create a light gray. Mix the two colors by kneading until you get a uniform color. Make a small ball, squash it with the tip of your finger, and then place it on the widest part of the head. This will create the snout.

Two small gray balls will make up the nostrils. Use a toothpick or a modeling tool that allows you to make the holes in the nostrils; also make a slit on the snout to give each unicorn a smiling mouth.

The eyes are very simple to create—just make two small black balls. The blush on the unicorn's cheeks is made with two crushed pink balls on each side of the snout. It's super easy!

I think a multicolored mane will look great, so make a pink strand, a blue strand, and a lilac strand (to make the lilac color, mix blue and pink in equal parts). Place the three strands centered on the head to form the bangs, but try to leave enough space on the sides to place the ears.

To form the ears, model two small white balls; you must make a drop shape and placed one on each side of the bangs.

Ok, now we have a horse with a punk look! So, let's turn it into a unicorn. 😶

What distinguishes unicorns from horses is the horn. Well . . . OK, and magic. But for now, it will be enough for us to put a small horn of Model Magic; notice that it is just a yellow point placed in the center of the bangs. Remember that this compound is slow drying, so you must wait twenty-four hours before the next step.

After twenty-four hours, our unicorns will have dried and hardened. Now is the time to glue them to the headphones. Be sure to use a glue that works on plastic. Mine is instant drying, so I only used one drop and I waited fifteen seconds.

These headphones look great! I think mine might even sound better now. Is this magic?

Unicorn Ice Cream Pen

I know, I'm obsessed with everything that looks sweet, but I can't resist! I thought about how I could decorate my pens so that they look fun, and then I thought: Why not turn them into ice cream cones?

The difficulty for this project is medium. To make one pen, you need to do at least one hour of work and let it dry for twenty-four hours.

Supplies:

- Model Magic (colors: yellow, white, pink, and black)
- Rolling pin and tools for modeling
- Pen
- Scissors
- Coarse salt
- Colored chalks (your favorite colors)
- Glitter (match the chalk colors above)
- White glue
- Liquid silicone glue
- Wooden stick
- Gold acrylic paint
- Pink permanent maker
- Soft brush

Instructions:

Whenever you use Model Magic or any other modeling dough, it is important that your hands are clean so that residual dirt from your hands doesn't get stuck in your mold. Begin by making the waffle cone. Make a yellow Model Magic ball that is approximately the size of a tennis ball. Use a roller to stretch it.

Make a cone shape that is as tall as your pen. You can use the scissors to cut the dough. Use a ruler or another flat tool to make lines that form the typical rhombuses in real waffle cones.

Take out the ink tube from the pen and wrap the plastic with the Model Magic cone. Try to make it look like a real ice cream cone. Remember that this modeling clay sticks to itself on contact, so you only have to join both ends of the cone so that they are fully stuck together. Let it dry for at least five hours.

Tip: To prevent your cone from warping while it dries, it is better to let it stand on its widest part.

To decorate the waffle, we will use salt. However, first you have to give the salt some color. Put a small amount of coarse salt on paper. Then take the chalk of the color you like the most and rub it over the salt so that it changes color. When all the salt has been colored, mix it with a little glitter of the same color.

Now that the cone has dried enough to maintain its shape, put white glue on the cone's opening and rim the cone in the salt/glitter mixture. Let the glue dry. When it is completely dry, it will become transparent.

Once the white glue is dry, it's time to move on to the next step. Put a bit of liquid silicone glue inside the the narrowest part of the cone and insert the pen so that it sticks. Fill the inside of the cone with Model Magic around the pen.

Let's make the ice cream scoop. Make a white Model Magic ball and place it just above the cone. If the ballpoint sticks out slightly, insert it inside the bottom of the white scoop. Press the ball so that it becomes stuck to the cone.

Mold a white Model Magic strand that is the length of the circumference of the ice cream scoop. Place it around the white ice cream scoop at the base.

To make unicorn ice cream, it is essential that we have a horn. Use any color of Model Magic because later we will paint it in a golden color. Roll a long strand on a wooden stick. The strand should start thicker at one end and decrease in size until it ends in a point. (Please reference the following image.) Then paint the horn with gold-colored acrylic paint.

The ice cream is ready; it seems so real. Let's transform it into unicorn ice cream.

To make the unicorn's ears, we will mold two white triangles out of Model Magic. Using the permanent marker, make a pink triangle inside of each ear. (You can also use pink paint for this step, if you don't have a permanent marker.)

Make several pink Model Magic strands and roll them to form the topping. Stick the topping right on top of the ice cream scoop. Then, stick the horn on top of the pink cream topping along with one ear on each side of the horn.

To finish the project, make a pair of black eyelashes with Model Magic. Place them on the ice cream scoop and apply a pink chalk blush to each cheek with a soft brush. Then let it dry for twenty-four hours before using it. To avoid the pen becoming warped while it dries, you can put it in a small glass. When it has dried, reinsert the ink mine, and it's ready to write with.

I assure you that you will have the most adorable pen around! 😍

Illuminate your dreams, and they will be magical!

Unicorn Lantern

I will show you how you can make a unicorn lamp from a recycled glass jar. You can place it on your bedside table so that it illuminates your room at night. This lantern is easy to make and fast, although it does take some time to dry. The whole process should take approximately two hours.

Supplies:

- Glass jar
- Unicorn silhouette
- Super glue
- White glue
- Turquoise glitter
- Sheet of paper
- Pink sequined ribbon
- Artificial flowers
- Scissors
- Paint sponge
- LED candle
- Hair spray

Instructions:

Save an empty glass jar; this craft is made from recycled goods.

You will also need the silhouette of a unicorn. You can either make this yourself or search for an image that you like on the Internet and print it to use as a template. Make sure the silhouette is smaller than your glass jar. If you decided to print it like I did, cut it out.

Then stick the unicorn inside the jar using a glue that sticks to glass. I used super glue that instantly dries. Do not use too much glue; a few drops will be enough.

With a paint sponge or a thick brush, spread a generous layer of white glue on the outside of the glass jar, excluding the bottom and the area where the lid would go. Don't worry if it looks too white; this type of glue becomes transparent when it dries.

Place a clean piece of paper on the table (it will be necessary to catch the excess glitter). Grab the jar by the lip that has no glue and sprinkle turquoise glitter all over the rest of the jar. All the glue must be completely covered with glitter, so recover what falls on the sheet of paper and throw it back on top of the glue. Then let it air dry. Once it's dried, coat the outside of the jar with hair spray so that the glitter does not fall off.

Once the lacquer has dried, you can decorate the area where the lid would have gone. Glue a strip of pink sequins around the outline (you can use any glue that sticks on glass). Take several turns until covering the entire thread of the jar.

Finally, paste a few artificial flowers to give the lantern a very colorful spring touch. All that remains after that is to put an LED candle inside and to turn it on whenever you want a little bit of magic light.

How beautiful is this lantern? I love it both on and off!

Make a garland of unicorn lanterns by recycling plastic cups.

Unicorn Lights Garland

Who would ever know that this beautiful garland of lights was made with reused plastic cups?

This idea occurred to me when Christmas was over and it was time to remove the Christmas tree. I always keep the lights in a box and put them in the attic until the following year, but this time I wanted to see those beautiful lights all year long. So I recycled the plastic cups from the party the night before and . . . *presto!* Do you love it? It is an easy craft and it takes about thirty minutes to complete.

Supplies:

- Disposable white plastic cups
- Garland of LED lights (it is important that the bulbs are LED since they do not heat up and thus decreases the risk of a fire)
- Scissors
- Pink and black permanent marker
- Golden cardboard
- Small cloth flowers
- Glue that sticks on plastic
- Pink silk paper
- Transparent tape

Instructions:

To make this garland, I have used disposable cups. Use as many cups as light bulbs that you have on your garland of lights. It is better to use a garland that has between ten and twelve bulbs.

Cut an X in the bottom of each cup. Through this cut, we will insert the light bulbs, but this will be in the final step. Also, cut off the strip of hard plastic around the mouth of the glass.

Use permanent markers to draw the unicorn's eyes and blush on each cup. I personally like how closed eyes look, and they are easier to draw than open, so I drew a couple of curved lines with several dashes for eyelashes. The rosy cheeks are two pink spots.

I know where I'll put my garland of unicorn lights. I'll put it on the headboard of my bed. #LongLiveTheUnicorns

Cut out triangles of golden cardboard (mine have glitter because I love everything that shines). These triangles will make up the horns of the unicorns. Paste them on using glue that sticks to the plastic. Also, paste three small artificial flowers at the base of each horn.

To finish, feed the light bulbs through the Xs that we cut at the beginning of the project. I have alternated using pink and unicorn cups for aesthetic purposes, but feel free to create any combination that you like!

To give the garland a little variation, some of the cups will be unicorns and others will simply be pink, which will need to be covered with pink silk paper. This type of paper is very thin and will allow light from the bulbs to shine through. Stick it around some of the cups with clear tape.

It's perfect for decorating a birthday party, too! 😜

Make school days more fun!

Unicorn Notebook

I finished my school days a few years ago, but I remember that I always decorated some of my notebooks. I especially liked to decorate them when they were newly bought and still had that "new smell." I'm not sure how to describe that smell, but I'm sure you know what I mean.

To decorate this notebook, I've been inspired by those apps with filters that recognize your face and transform it into characters that interact with gestures. I especially like the one that makes a rainbow come out of your mouth and gives you big kawaii-style eyes and rosy cheeks. It makes me laugh! 😂

This craft is easy and can be finished in approximately thirty minutes.

Supplies:

- Notebook
- Sheet of white cardboard
- Glue stick
- White and gold (with glitter) foam paper
- Liquid silicone glue
- Pink permanent maker (also you can use pink acrylic paint)
- Marker pens (colors: black, pink, orange, yellow, blue, green, purple, and red)
- Colorful pompoms
- Compass
- Scissors
- White acrylic paint
- Pink chalk
- Soft brush
- Pencil

Instructions:

It's possible that at this point in the book you've already realized that I love unicorns! That's why my notebook will be a cute kawaii-style unicorn that looks like the rainbow filter on your phone!

Cut out a sheet of white cardboard to be the same size as the notebook you want to decorate and paste it to the cover with a glue stick.

Use white foam paper to make the unicorn's ears and stick them to the notebook with liquid silicone glue. Inside the ears, make some pink triangles to add depth. You can do this with a permanent marker or with pink acrylic paint. The horn of the unicorn is a gold glitter triangle of foam paper; stick it between the two ears also using liquid silicone.

To decorate the front of the unicorn, I will use colored pompoms. These pompoms are very soft, exist in many sizes, and are available in craft stores everywhere. Combine different-colored pompoms and stick them with liquid silicone.

We are going to draw big, round eyes in kawaii style. To make them perfect, use a compass (or a similarly sized round object) and then color the inside with a black marker. Leave a couple of uncolored circles inside each eye. This will create the typical shimmer found in kawaii eyes. Use the black marker again to draw a mouth shaped like the number three lying down. Place the mouth between both eyes.

Use colored markers to draw a rainbow that comes out of the unicorn's mouth. It will be easier to center if you first trace the lines with a pencil, then color it with the markers.

Then, paint crosses and dots with white acrylic paint along the entire rainbow. This will create the light flashes. As a final touch, you can paint rosy cheeks with chalk, but be sure to apply it using a soft brush to make it fade.

What kind of unicorn would it be if it couldn't sneeze out a rainbow?

Design your own pencil case!

Unicorn Pencil Case

I love to draw. Whenever I have some leisure time, I take my pencil and draw anything that pops into my mind. If I'm being honest, I'm not very good at drawing, but I don't care—I love it.

These days, I can only think of unicorns. Has anyone else noticed this? I drew a unicorn face and it occurred to me that I could transform that drawing into a case to store my pencils. This craft can be completed in one afternoon, in approximately three hours plus the drying time, and has a high level of difficulty.

Supplies:

- 4 sheets of paper
- Scissors
- Masking tape
- Felt colors (your preference)
- A magnetic closure for bags
- Liquid silicone glue

Instructions:

The first thing is to draw your own design on a sheet of paper. It is important to anticipate the size of the pencils that you will put inside the case and to make the drawing ¾ inch bigger so that the pencils will fit appropriately.

Another thing to keep in mind is the part of the drawing that you will use as a cover. For my case, it will be the mane, so I drew a big mane on my unicorn. If you do not feel inspired to design your own case, you can also imitate the one I made while still incorporating elements of your own style.

I'm going to teach you how to create your own template. This will help you make different pieces of your case, but also be very useful in making your own templates for other projects. You will need several sheets of paper. The main concept behind creating a template is tracing the separate parts of your drawing individually.

If you look at the following image, you can see that I have traced the outline of the face individually on a piece of paper. I have also traced the horn,

eyes, ears, and blush. On another sheet of paper, I have traced the different parts of the bangs and the snout. In summary, trace each component individually and cut it out.

Stick each piece on its corresponding felt color with masking tape. This is a trick that I use to avoid having to draw the pieces on the felt and thus not risk getting pencil marks on it. Then cut out the outline with the scissors. Please note that the cream-colored pieces that correspond to the head and face have a particularity. I will explain how to create them in the next step.

I have decided to make the case with a double layer of felt so that it's more robust. It also serves to hide the closure between both layers of felt, but this can be seen more clearly in later steps. As I mentioned previously, the cream-colored pieces that correspond to the head and face have a particularity that makes them distinguishable from one another.

The larger pieces correspond to the back of the case, and have protruding trapezoid shapes at the top (above the unicorn's bangs). This trapezoid is where you are going to stick the bangs. This will also serve as the mechanism where the case will open and close.

The smaller cream-colored face pieces will make up the front of the case. Notice that the bottom contour is the same shape as the back piece, but the top is cut at the base of the ears. I have cut double layers for the unicorn's bangs and its horn, but for the pink zone of the ears, the eyes, the blush, and the snout, I have only made single cuts.

Now, we begin to form the case. Use liquid silicone to stick it together. First, glue the pieces that make up the back of the case. These are the larger cream-colored pieces.

Next, separately join the pieces that will be the front of the case, leaving the top end open where you will place the magnetic closure. This is so the closure's "legs" are hidden between both fabrics.

This kind of closure has two pieces that are joined together by magnets. The pieces each have two "legs" that must be inserted into the fabric, so make two small cuts in the first layer of felt. Next feed the "legs" through these cuts and close the inside of the fabric. Join both fabrics with liquid silicone glue.

Then place both cream-colored pieces together and join them with a thin line of liquid silicone glue all along the edge of the lower contour, forming the bag that will house the pencils. Be sure to leave the top part open or you won't have anywhere to put the pencils!

Place the other part of the closure on the piece of the bangs that is in direct contact with the face. Before making the cuts where you should insert the closure, make sure that the bangs are in their correct position so that all the pieces fit together perfectly. Then join both parts of the magnetic closure and adjust this piece of the bangs to its proper position. Pull the trapezoid piece forward and glue the bangs and magnetic closure to it.

Once it has dried, remove the weight and paste the rest of the pieces, guiding yourself with your original drawing. Then let it dry and your case will be ready.

Then paste on top the other twin piece, hiding the trapezoid and the closure between both pieces of the bangs. Let these pieces dry before continuing. Remember that liquid silicone takes a few minutes to dry, so I recommend putting weight on the case while it dries (I used a heavy book).

OOOH! Have you ever seen such a lovely pencil holder?

Cloud Unicorn Pencil Holder

I am somewhat disorganized. My table sometimes looks like a flea market for school supplies and the worst thing is that I can never find the pencil that I want to use. I need to get rid of my bad habits. I promise to organize my desk, but for this I need a beautiful pencil holder, so I'll make one myself! Let me think . . . what if it were . . . a unicorn cloud?

Supplies:

- Sheet of paper
- Pencil
- Scissors
- Ruler
- Glue
- Gray carton board (⅒ inch thick)
- Acrylic paints
- Brush
- Black permanent marker

Instructions:

This pencil holder will be 100 percent your own design. This means that it will be as you imagine it, both in size and shape.

We will start by drawing the design on a sheet of paper. In my case, I have chosen a unicorn cloud shape, but take the liberty of drawing whatever you like. Just keep in mind that the base needs to be wide enough keep standing, so do not make circular or pointy shapes in the lower part of the drawing.

Or, if you prefer, you can try to imitate my design. It's very easy! As you can see in the following image, I have occupied the entire width of the paper with my drawing, so it will be big enough to hold all my pencils.

Take a pair of scissors and cut your drawing around the perimeter. This will be used as a template. Then place your template on the cardboard, hold it with one hand so it does not move, and with a pencil trace the outline on the cardboard. Draw it twice. These identical cut-outs will make up the front and the back of our pencil holder.

Cut out both cardboard shapes. This type of cardboard can be somewhat hard, so you will need strong scissors (and possibly the help of an adult).

> **Tip:** To be exact, you can cut leaving a small margin and sand the cardboard with a medium grain sandpaper until you reach the outline of the drawing.

Once you have two pieces of cardboard (which should be the same size), outline the areas where you want to divide the pencil holder. First, draw a straight line on the base and then draw some vertical lines that serve as guides for the dividers. For my design, I've divided it into three, which I think is the perfect ratio for my cloud.

Measure the lines you have drawn and cut some pieces of cardboard with those dimensions. In my case, the bottom of each piece is approximately two inches. Be sure to measure both the height and width!

Now cut out each divider and line up each on the pencil line that corresponds to it. Glue them in place (you can use white glue or any glue that sticks to cardboard).

Great! The hard work is done and now comes the most fun: painting!

Finally, put glue on each of the edges of the dividers and place the other half of the cloud on top. Try to match the exact position with the back so that when you stand it up, it balances.

Add some color to your design. Start by painting everything white and letting it dry. Then, you can trace with a pencil the rest of the details so it will be much easier to paint.

For my cloud design, I decided to go over all the contours with a black permanent marker so it would be easy for me to paint inside the lines.

Now that all the contours are drawn with a marker, it is much easier to fill each area with its respective color. You can use a fine brush to avoid going outside the lines and make sure that your design looks flawless. Notice that I have painted a blue strip around the contour. Adding details are a very nice touch that gives your design depth and character. If you make a mistake and accidentally paint outside of the lines, don't worry: you can always paint over it with white and redo the section. The important thing here is to have fun!

Remember that before using the pencil holder, it is necessary to let the paint dry for a few hours. It might be a good idea to let it dry until the next day. And *Voilá!* Don't you think it's amazing that we have created this wonderful pencil holder from a piece of cardboard?

Dear pencil, I will never lose sight of you again. 😎

Why not personalize your phone case?

Unicorn DIY Phone Case

Okay, I'm beginning to suspect that I have an obsession with collecting phone cases. I have more than twenty different cases, all of which I made with my own hands. The truth is that what I like most about creating my own phone cases is the time it takes to make the case—and, of course, the selfie in the mirror when it's finished!

In this chapter, I will teach you how to customize your phone case(s) in an easy and creative way. For this project, your case will become a unicorn. This craft is relatively easy and will only take you thirty minutes plus drying time.

Supplies:

- Rigid phone case
- Model Magic (colors: white, fuchsia, yellow, blue, and black)
- Rolling pin for kneading
- Ruler
- Scissors
- Liquid silicone glue

Instructions:

Take a little fuchsia Model Magic, make a ball about the size of a kiwi (more or less), and flatten it with a rolling pin. You will need to roll a sheet of Model Magic that is approximately ⅕-inch thick and is slightly larger than the phone case you are going to decorate.

With the help of a ruler, cut the dough as neatly as possible. This cut will be the division between the unicorn's white face and its fuchsia snout, so it must be quite straight. Repeat the same steps you have done so far, but using white Model Magic.

Join both colors on the straight edge that you cut with the ruler. The overall sheet of dough must be slightly larger than your phone case.

You already know that pieces of Model Magic stick to each other on contact. However, it doesn't stick so well to plastic, so to cover the phone case, it is necessary to apply liquid silicone glue all over the outer surface of the case. Don't forget to apply glue on the sides of the case as well!

Then carefully place the case in the center of the Model Magic sheet, ensuring that the dividing line of both colors is in the center of the sleeve. Fold up the sides. Then trim off all the excess dough with scissors and soften the edges with your fingers.

The cover is now ready to decorate like a unicorn. To make the horn, I have attached three strands of pink, white, and lilac Model Magic (the lilac color can be obtained by mixing pink dough with blue dough). Then twist the strands as shown in the following image and then cut through the base area with the scissors so that the horn measures approximately 1 ¼ inch in height.

The rest of the pieces that make up the unicorn's face are very simple to make. Look at the following image: the ears will be formed by two white triangles and two smaller pink triangles. The eyes consist of two black Model Magic ovals and the unicorn's bangs are made up of a variety of multi-colored Model Magic strands.

Place each piece in its appropriate place to form the face of the unicorn. Remember that this type of clay sticks to itself on contact; you must be precise. Once they touch, they will not be able to be separated. Finally, mark a shape similar to a "G" in the area of the nose. You can use the back of a fine brush to do it.

Do not forget to hollow out the section where the phone's camera is as well as the rest of the holes in the case, i.e. charging port, volume controls, etc. You can use small scissors to do this.

A nice unicorn will hold onto my savings!

Papier-Mâché Unicorn Piggy Bank

#UnicornPiggyBank #UnicornPaperMache #IsasUnicornCrafts

Papier-mâché is one of the most-loved techniques in crafts. It is incredible to think that, from paper and glue, you can create beautiful figures. For this project, I designed a nice baby unicorn piggy bank where we can keep our coins. This papier-mâché unicorn is easy to make, but requires a lot of drying time (about three days), so make it a weekend project.

Supplies:

- 2 balloons
- Scotch tape
- White glue
- Instant glue (super glue)
- Water
- Paper towel
- Diary paper
- Brush
- Scissors
- Pencil
- Black permanent marker
- Silicone or cork stopper
- Acrylic paints: white, blue, pink, and yellow

Instructions:

For this papier-mâché piggy bank, the inside needs to be hollow to save the coins. So, we will use balloons as a mold and then remove them when the project is finished.

Inflate two balloons and tie them. One balloon must be larger to serve as the mold for the unicorn's body and the other balloon should be smaller to create the head.

Join them using adhesive tape. Try to place them in the shape of a unicorn. Also, put adhesive tape around the conjoining area of the balloons, forming the neck of the unicorn.

Tip: It's possible that you have thought to accelerate the drying process with a hair dryer, but this is a serious mistake because the dryer would heat the air inside the balloons, causing them to increase in size so much that they pop and destroy the project or fluxuate back-and-forth from their normal size between heating and cooling, thus ruining the shape of the papier-mâché. (I'm afraid I learned this from my own experience.) 😭

It's time to make papier-mâché, this technique consists of sticking pieces of paper onto a mold with a mixture of glue and water. After several layers and some drying time, the shell becomes very hard, opening a new world of countless projects.

Mix white glue and water in a bowl. You should use approximately 70 percent glue and 30 percent water. Rip some pieces of paper towel and use a brush to glue them all over the surface of the balloons, being sure to leave no empty spaces. To make it easier to apply, you can use containers to support the balloons while you work. Then let the mold air dry for at least six hours.

When those six hours have passed, apply again another layer of paper and let them dry all night.

To make the legs, ears, horn, hair, and tail of the unicorn, I used newspaper. Form four balls and glue them, using quick glue, to the lower part of the body. These will be the legs. Remember to leave a large gap between the four legs that will be where we will remove the coins later.

Repeat the same process to create the horn, the ears, the hair, and the tail, and glue them in place. Leave a tiny slit in the head (behind the horn) where you can put your coins. If you prefer, you can do this in the upper part of the body instead.

Reapply a new layer of papier-mâché and let it dry until the next day.

As a cover for the coin area, you can use a silicone plug or a cork stopper. The one that I used is silicone. I have repurposed it from an empty face cream jar. You can probably find a jar of cream that carries this type of flexible cap. If you can't find one, you can buy a cork stopper that is approximately 1 ⅕ inches in diameter. With a pencil, draw the outline of the plug in the lower part of the unicorn's body and trim it with the scissors, then make sure that the plug fits perfectly. Remove the balloons through that hole.

Make sure the hole you left on the head or back is large enough to fit the type of coins you'd like to save.

Now, it is time for the most fun part of any craft: paint time! Use acrylic paints to bring the piggy bank to life. Paint the body and ears white, the horn and legs yellow, and alternate pink and blue for the mane and tail.

Fabulous! With papier-mâché, you can make many great crafts, just give free rein to your imagination and create your own figures.

Is there a better way to decorate your room than with a unicorn pillow?

Unicorn Pillow

I wanted to decorate my room with things that I made with my own hands and thought I could make a unique pillow to place on my bed. Only, I didn't want the typical boring pillow. I thought to myself: *Why not make a unicorn pillow?* For this project, I'll teach you how to make your own pillow that will make you have magical dreams.

If you're wondering how long it took me to make my pillow, I started on a Saturday morning and it was ready before lunch time! The difficulty of this craft is medium. As always, when you sew something, it is better to ask for help from someone who has more experience.

Supplies:

- Microfiber cushion or supersoft plush fabric (white)
- Filling for cushion
- White thread and needle
- Felt fabric (colors: black, yellow, pink, fuchsia, lilac, orange, red, and turquoise)
- Scissors
- Pencil
- Paper
- Liquid silicone glue

Instructions:

To start, you have two options to choose from:

1. You can get a white cushion with supersoft microfiber and customize it. This option is the easiest and you don't need to sew.

2. As a second option, you can make your own cushion, but to do this you have to sew.

In this case, I have chosen option 2 to show you how it's done.

For this option, you will need to purchase supersoft microfiber. If you haven't heard of this, have you seen those incredibly soft sofa blankets? It's that kind of fabric. It can be found in fabric stores or on the Internet.

On a table, place two equally-sized pieces of cloth, one on top of the other. Make sure they are flat!

With a pencil, draw a square on the canvas. Mine is 15 ¾ inches x 15 ¾ inches. This size is the most common cushion size, which is why I chose these measurements.

Take a needle and some white thread and sew the entire contour of the cushion, just above the pencil mark, but leave a gap to stuff the pillow.

You must leave a hole large enough to stuff the pillow with the cushion filling. Turn the fabric and start filling it.

Once the pillow is completely stuffed, finish sewing the hole closed. Now, we can go and create the decoration to transform it into a beautiful unicorn cushion.

Next, take a needle and some white thread and sew over the pencil mark, leaving the part of the base unsewn.

Flip the fabric and fill the ears with stuffing. Insert enough filling so that they are sufficiently stuffed.

Next, we are going to make the unicorn's ears. To make sure that both ears are the same size, draw an ear shape on a piece of paper (a triangle with two rounded sides). Cut it out to serve as a template. The ears that I have drawn have an approximate height of 4 inches and in their widest part 2 ½ inches (they are not exact measurements, but it will help you to get an idea for sizing). On a double layer of cloth, trace the ear with your pencil. Remember to make two identical ears.

WOW! How soft is this cushion? Suddenly I feel a little sleepy, but NO! "Isa, don't be lazy." I'll finish my cushion before lunch.

On pink felt fabric, trace a triangle shape again. Make this template ¼ inch smaller than the previous ear template, which should provide enough of a margin to create the inner layer of the ear. Cut out two pink felt pieces using the template and glue one in each ear. You can use liquid silicone glue. Let it dry completely.

To make the roses that adorn the mane of this unicorn, we will use all different colors of felt. Cut out several circles, measuring 4 ¾ inches in diameter. Next, cut the circle in a spiral. In the following image, you can see that I drew the spiral with a pencil. However, if possible, try to cut the circle without drawing an outline beforehand, so there will be no pencil marks. If you find it difficult, try to make the pencil stroke very light, so it's not too visible.

Roll the spiral up, starting from the outside and finishing at the center of the circle. Use liquid silicone glue to paste the circular shape to the front top center of the pillow, just below where you will also place the unicorn's horn. Press each for at least thirty seconds so that they are properly glued, and let them dry completely. Repeat the same process with all the circles to form six roses of different colors.

Great, almost finished! And I can only think how comfortable it will be to nap on this pillow. 😴

On yellow felt, draw a cone with a height of 4 ¾ inches. If you want, you can draw it first on a piece of paper and use it as a template. After tracing it on the felt, cut it out.

Fold the cone in half and sew it along the two straight edges to form the horn. Be sure to leave the top of the cone open. Then fill it with cushion filling, using enough to keep it firm and standing when you glue it to the cushion.

To make the eyes, I used black felt. It is very simple, just cut out a curved shape with three tabs for the eyelashes. Now, that we have all the components finished, you just have to stick them with liquid silicone glue.

It is finally finished! It's soo soft . . . You can't stop hugging it. 😘

I don't know if it's sweeter inside or out!

Mini Unicorn Piñata

#UnicornPinata #UnicornParty #HappyBirthdayToMe
#InLoveWithSweets #IsasUnicornCrafts

I had never made a piñata prior to writing this book, so I thought that for my first attempt making a small one was better. However, after finishing it, I realized that to make a big one is just as easy. So I think next time I'll do it big. I'm already preparing for my next party!

This is an easy craft, but it's still time consuming. I'm sure it will take you at least an entire afternoon to finish. If you decide to make a giant piñata, it will surely take you a whole day. But the result is incredible!

Supplies:

- Cardboard
- Masking tape
- White glue
- Pencil
- Scissors
- Rope
- Crepe paper (colors: white, blue, pink, yellow, and purple)
- Colored cardstock (colors: white, black, light pink, gold with glitter, and pink with glitter)

Instructions:

You will need two cardboard circles that are approximately 8 inches in diameter and a very long strip of cardboard that is 26 inches in length and 4 inches in width. Roll the long strip up, making sure the lines in the cardboard run horizontally. Find an object with a cylindrical shape and use it to roll the long strip of cardboard.

Use masking tape pieces to join the cardboard strip to the contour of one of the circles. Leave the last 4 inches free. This will act as the lid for the piñata. Trim any overlap. Then place the other circle on the opposite side and repeat the process.

Bend back the 4 inches of loose cardboard (the lid) where you will fill the piñata.

Like all piñatas, it must be hung so children can hit it and make the candy fall out. Therefore, you must put a string on it. With the tip of a sharp pencil, pierce the cardboard, making a hole on each side of the lid, then insert a string and knot it on the inside. Once it's been filled with your desired candies or goodies, put a piece of masking tape to close the piñata.

Glue the crepe paper to the piñata using white glue. Make sure that all sides of the piñata are completely covered with crepe paper, including the lid.

It's time for decorating! As with every project, this is the most fun part!

Use crepe paper to decorate the piñata. Take a double-layered strip of white crepe paper about 1⅕ inch wide and make vertical cuts with your scissors. Do not cut all the way through the strip. You can use the next image for reference.

Awesome! If I realized earlier in my life that making a piñata was sooo easy, I assure you that I would have built one for each one of my birthdays.

The unicorn's eyes, ears, blush, and horn will be made with colored cardstock. The shapes are easy to create: just draw them on the cardstock, cut them out, and then glue them to the piñata using white glue.

For the horn and the insides of the ears, I used glitter cardboard, which gives the piñata a more glamorous look.

The unicorn hair is also made with colored crepe paper. Cut it into many strips and stick them around the horn and ears with white glue.

Did you think it would be possible to make
a stuffed unicorn using socks?

Unicorn Plush Toy

#UnicornPlush #MyBestFriendIsAUnicorn
#IMakeMyOwnStuffedAnimals #IsasUnicornCrafts

When I was six years old, I accompanied my older sister Lorena to her friend's house. My sister and her friend were going to do homework together, and I endeavored to tag along.

When we entered her friend's room, she had a bed full of dolls, and I was impressed. I said, "Wow, how many dolls do you have?" and I thought that her parents must be millionaires.

Then she knelt at the foot of her bed and pulled out a large box from below. She opened the box and inside there were pieces of cloth, wool, stuffed animals, and many colors of yarn. She explained that her mother did not have money to buy dolls, so she made her own dolls out of pieces of clothing that were too small for her.

That experience inspired me to make this beautiful unicorn plush doll. To make this doll, it is necessary to sew, so we can say that this craft is a high level of difficulty. I advise you to ask for help from an adult or someone who may have more experience with sewing.

Supplies:

- 3 fluffy socks (2 pink and 1 white)
- Scissors
- Marker (different color than the socks)
- Thread and needle
- Cushion filling
- Glossy golden fabric
- Foam paper (pink glitter and black)
- Felt fabric (green turquoise, pink, and lilac)
- Liquid silicone glue

Instructions:

Get three fluffy socks. The size of your stuffed animal will depend on the size of socks you use; the bigger the sock, the bigger the doll.

In the following image, you can see how you have to divide the socks to create the different parts of the unicorn's body. The black lines in the image indicate where to cut and the white dotted lines indicate where to sew.

Don't worry if you're not good at sewing. I'm not good either, but the fabric of these socks will hide any defect or mistake in the seams!

Begin with the body (center of image). Flip the first fuchsia sock inside out. Looking at the image, draw the dotted line with a marker, so it will be easier to sew. Now, take a needle, thread it, and sew over the line. This is how you will form the unicorn's legs.

Cut along the imaginary straight black line between both legs to separate them. Be careful not to cut the seam that you just made. Also, cut the sock toe along the line indicated in the same diagram on this page. Through that hole, you can flip the sock right side out.

In the same way, take the other fuchsia sock and sew the arms. Then, cut the arms and the rest of the pieces as indicated. Follow the lines of the first image to guide you.

Fill the body of the unicorn with cushion stuffing until you can't fit any more. The socks' fabric is elastic, so it will increase in size as you introduce the filling and can stretch a considerable amount.

It is time to close the body. Use a needle and double thread to sew it. Please note that you will need a resistant thread. Make a very simple zig-zag seam. Sew all around the contour until reaching the starting point. Easy, right?

Now, pull the strand of thread and you will notice that the fabric has gathered and the hole is closed. Take advantage when the hole is still small and introduce more filling to increase your unicorn's size, then sew the hole from side to side to close it.

At this point, you would have ideally sewn and cut the arms from the second sock. For each arm, flip the fabric right-side out so that the seams are inside, stuff the arms with filling, and sew the holes closed. Then, sew an arm on each side of the body as seen in the following image, using as much thread as you need to secure the arms.

Reference again the first image containing the diagrams. The toe of the second fuchsia sock will be the head of the unicorn. Stuff it with filling and sew it shut, as you did with the body, with double thread and zig-zag stitching around the contour. Then sew from side-to-side to close it completely.

Once you have your head ready, sew it to the body. Remember: you can use all the thread you want; it is important that the head is firmly fixed to the body.

Take the white sock and cut the toe according to the diagram on page 100. This will be the unicorn's snout. Position it on the lower part of the face and sew the whole contour leaving a small hole to stuff it with filling. Once you have filled it in, finish sewing the hole closed.

Now we have the base of the doll. At this point, you could really transform it into any animal, but for this project, it will be a beautiful fuchsia unicorn.

Next, we're going to make the horn. I think many unicorns have a golden horn, so ours should have one, too! On a piece of shiny gold cloth, draw a cone shape about 1 ½ inches high and cut it using your outline as a guide, leaving a margin of about ⅕ inch.

With the fabric that you have left over from the second fuchsia sock, cut two triangle shapes to form the ears, sew them (leaving the small end open), and turn the fabric so that the seams stay inside. If necessary, fill them a bit so they stay straight. Then, sew one on each side of the head,

Bend the triangle in half so it forms a cone and stitch along the radius you've drawn, leaving a slight overlap. Don't sew the mouth of the cone closed! Next, flip the fabric right side out and fill the cone with stuffing to form the horn.

To make the eyes, nose, and mouth, we will use black and pink glitter foam paper. Cut out the shape of two eyes closed with eyelashes, a pair of pink hearts that will be the nose, and a smiling mouth. To stick them to the face, you can use liquid silicone glue. I advise you to put a small amount of silicone, so that it looks much cleaner and does not spill out.

Now sew the horn right in the center of the head. Do not worry if you see the seams because will be covered with the unicorn's bangs.

To make the unicorn's belly, we will cut a piece of the white sock. In this case, you will need an oval shape. Using white thread (so the seam is hidden), sew it on the front of the body.

For the finishing touches, we need to add the bangs, mane, and tail to this beautiful unicorn. We will use felt fabric in a variety of different colors to trace and cut out some undulating shapes. You can imitate the shapes that I used for my unicorn.

Then glue the felt with liquid silicone to your unicorn. Remember to put some nice bangs on the front of the unicorn's head, a healthy mane on the back of its head, and a curvy tail on its back. Combine several colors to make it look more beautiful.

Now it's ready. You learned how to make your own stuffed unicorn; if you wanted, you could make many unicorns of many different colors and fill your bed with unicorns like my sister's friend with her dolls. 😊

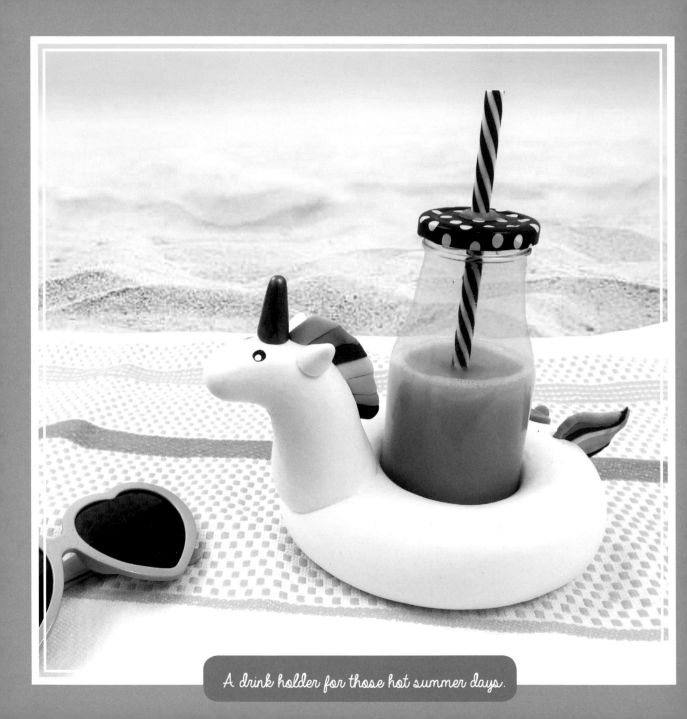

A drink holder for those hot summer days.

Miniature Unicorn Floating Cupholder

#UnicornFloat #UnicornCupHolder #IsasUnicornCrafts

Last summer, I saw these things everywhere. Everyone published photos on Instagram with their beautiful floating unicorn, and I had no choice but to devise a project inspired by this trend.

But as you know, I feel the need for my crafts to not only be beautiful, but also be useful. So, thinking back to my beach and pool days past, I remembered how many times I spilled my soda on my towel because grass and sand are not the most stable surfaces to rest your drink.

That's why I made this unicorn float that holds your drink. The cupholder is easy to make and will take approximately an hour plus drying time to complete.

Supplies:

- Model Magic (colors: white, yellow, fuchsia, blue, green, red, and gray)
- Glass
- Gold and white acrylic paints
- Black permanent marker
- Transparent acrylic lacquer spray

Instructions:

You already know that an essential part of working with Model Magic is to have very clean hands, since it is a modeling compound where any particles of dirt will stick. For this project, we will use mostly white Model Magic, so before starting, wash and dry your hands.

You need a lot of white Model Magic. I used approximately 12 ½ ounces. Roll a large ball, using the following image as a reference, so it's big enough to occupy the two palms of your hands. I used roughly 10 ½ ounces of the white Model Magic to make this ball.

Model the ball into a donut shape with your hands. To do this, lightly squeeze it and push one of your fingers through the center of the ball to create a hole, then continue modeling and smoothing the surface.

The hole in the donut has to be large enough to hold a glass, so once you think you have the right measurement, put the donut on a table and rest a glass in it. That glass will remain inside the float during the entire drying process.

Reserve a small amount of white Model Magic and then make the ears. With the remaining dough, make a thick strand that will make up the neck and head of the unicorn. Make the strand wider at the base and thinner at the top, then fold the top to form the head. Stick the whole piece to the donut. Model Magic sticks on contact, so just touch the pieces together and they will stick.

It is time to put the ears on this unicorn. Make small cones of white Model Magic and stick one on each side of the head, leaving enough separation between them to place the horn.

The hair and tail of the unicorn must have a variety of colors, so make multi-colored strands and join them together. Then, with a tool or a ruler, cut them into their respective shapes and stick them to the float.

Next, make a cone shape with yellow Model Magic. This will be the horn. Place it between the two ears just before the beginning of the hair, then paint it golden with acrylic paint.

Next, make a circle with gray Model Magic that will simulate the inflation valve. You can use the lid of the permanent marker to give it some texture. Then use the black permanent marker to draw a pair of eyes and white acrylic paint to paint a small dot inside each eye.

Let the float dry. Unfortunately, the drying process is very slow because the project requires a substantial amount of Model Magic. Remember to place the glass inside the unicorn to maintain dough's shape and let it dry for three days.

Once the Model Magic has dried, apply some varnish acrylic spray and let it dry for as long as the manufacturer recommends. This will protect the Model Magic from possible water exposure during the days at the beach or pool.

Tip: Due to the weight of the dough, it is possible for the unicorn head to bend, so I advise you to find some type of support. I used a glass that had the perfect height to place underneath the snout.

Reuse materials and care for the environment.

Unicorn Recycled Desk Organizer

There is just one thing I like more than doing crafts, and that is doing crafts with recycled materials. I love transforming something that would otherwise be thrown out into some artform.

It will be very useful to have a place to put my notebooks and papers; a nice unicorn will help me to keep everything organized.

Save a cereal box to transform it into a desk organizer; you can do this in less than an hour, and it's very easy.

Supplies:

- Cereal box
- Pencil
- Ruler
- Scissors
- Acrylic paints
- Brush
- Decorated paper
- Glue stick
- Fabric flower (optional)

Instructions:

For this project, we will reuse a cereal box. Most cereals boxes are brightly colored, but can usually be completely covered with a thick enough paint. It's better to paint the entire box with a light color. I have chosen very light pink.

Once the paint has dried, draw the shape you want your organizer to have using a pencil and a ruler. For mine, I drew a unicorn face on the front and raised the backdrop, but you can make the design however you like! If you choose to use my design, first you must draw the outline of the ears and the horn.

For the next step, cut the cardboard box along the pencil line. Take your time to be exact. As my mom always says, "Hurrying is not a good companion."

Then, break out your acrylic paints and your brush and paint your box to look like a unicorn. I'm going to give my unicorn colorful bangs, closed eyes with big eyelashes, and pink blush on each cheek.

As a final touch, I pinned a fabric flower to the unicorn's bangs. It's super cute!

Decorate the inside of the box using decorated paper. This type of paper is traditionally used in scrapbooking, so you can find it in any craft store. Choose one that complements the colors you have used to paint the outside of the box. Use a glue stick to paste it to the box.

Ok, this was too easy, but it looks adorable!

Keep your secrets inside this magic book.

Unicorn Fantasy Secret Book

Everyone will think it's a fantasy storybook—with magical unicorn stories, castles, and princesses. But no one will suspect that it is actually a false book where you can keep your treasures hidden.

This is a medium difficulty craft. We must pay special attention to the measurements of the pieces of cardboard (Note: For this project, I have used centimeters and millimeters as units of measurement to be exact). This is one of the most laborious projects in this book, so you should set aside a weekend for it, since it will take you a couple of days to complete.

Supplies:

- Cardboard (5 millimeters thick)
- Cardboard tube (what's left of a paper towel roll when it's all been used)
- Masking tape
- Glue: liquid silicone, glue stick, white glue, and super glue
- Fantasy-style image, printed 11 centimeters x 13 centimeters
- Foil
- White silk paper
- Acrylic paints
- Synthetic moss and some artificial flowers
- Brush
- Pencil
- Water varnish

Instructions:

This craft is a perfect excuse to reuse an old cardboard box. As I've mentioned in previous projects, I love using recycled materials for crafts. Whenever I can, I try to include these materials. For this project, I will use recycled cardboard that is 5 millimeters thick. In the following image, I have outlined the appropriate measurements in centimeters to be exact. It is important to be precise in this step so that the result looks realistic.

First, form a rectangle using two 17 x 5 centimeter pieces of cardboard and the two 14 x 5 centimeter pieces. Stick them together using liquid silicone glue. Remember that liquid silicone takes a few minutes to dry, so be patient.

While these pieces dry, use masking tape to cover the edges of the other cardboard pieces. This will cover the inner ridges of the cardboard so that they are no longer visible. Once the rectangle from the previous step has dried, you should also cover the edges with masking tape.

Then paste the first rectangle you made to one of the 20 x 15 centimeter pieces of cardboard. You must align it with the left edge, and for the rest of the sides there should be 1 centimeter of overhang left. To glue the cardboard, use liquid silicone glue.

Reserve the remaining 20 x 15 centimeter piece. With the other smaller pieces, form the interior compartments. Glue them with liquid silicone.

Use masking tape to create the special hinge that will connect the lid with the rest of the book. This will allow it to open and close with ease. To do this, cut an 18-centimeter piece of masking tape and use it to join the book to the front of the cover. Position it so that it's level with the base and run your fingers over it several times so that it is firmly stuck in place.

Now, open the lid slowly until it forms a 180-degree angle and stick another strip of masking tape inside. Again, pass your fingers over the tape several times so that it adheres well.

I'm impressed. This already looks like a book. Now we will turn it into a magical book!

Surely you have noticed that old, robust books containing hundreds of pages have a curved spine. We will give that shape to our book so that it looks more realistic. To create this shape, use a cardboard tube—I used the inside of a paper towel roll that I reserved once I ran out of paper.

Cut the cardboard tube lengthwise and place it on the back of your book to measure how it will fit on the book's spine and mark the appropriate cut marks. Cut the paper towel roll according to the marks you've made.

Place the cardboard tube half just on the edge of the front cover and join it with masking tape. Repeat the same process with the back cover.

Find a unicorn image that you like. You can search for it on the Internet and print it out, use a cutout from a magazine, or you can even draw it yourself. This image must be approximately 11 centimeters x 13 centimeters. Paste it in the center of the book cover using the glue stick.

Use foil to make the raised strands on the front of the book as well as other shapes for aesthetic relief. Foil is great for making 3-D shapes. It sticks with super glue.

On the spine of the book, I have made elongated shapes simulating raised bands. Additionally, I have highlighted certain parts, trying to form stones and vegetation. It's not very appealing right now, but when it's finished it will look great.

Well done. This project has been pretty tough so far. That's why you deserve a break. Use the drying time to do something fun!

In the next step, I will try to unify all the protruding details of the book using white silk paper. To apply the silk paper, you must mix white glue with a little water. Make sure the glue maintains its consistency.

Cut pieces of silk paper and stick them to the raised details on the front cover. Avoid sticking paper on top of the unicorn image. Once it has dried, stick silk paper also on the back cover and inside the book as well. Do not stick it on the sides.

We are trying to add textures, so don't worry if the paper is wrinkled. That is precisely what we need. Keep the book cover open while it dries. This may take two to three hours. Otherwise, if you close it, it may stick, sealing the book shut.

Once the silk paper is dry, it's time to start painting. Use acrylic paints for this project. To unify the colors, apply white as a base color. Be careful not to paint the image that you pasted on the cover.

Paint the area that simulates the pages of the book with a cream color; you can also add some lines with gray to make them look like real sheets of paper.

I've tried to incorporate the unicorn image colors into the rest of the project, so I used colors like fuchsia, blue, lilac, and turquoise. In this step, don't worry too much about the details since the colors are going to mix in this section anyway. Once this has dried, you can be more precise in trying to paint the gray stones and green vegetation. I used several shades of each color to create a sensation of depth. Also paint the inside of the book and wait for it to dry.

I love this craft. It's so cute and looks like a magic book where I can keep my treasures safely hidden.

To finish the project, stick a bit of synthetic moss between the stones and add some artificial flowers wherever it seems fit. Apply a layer of water varnish to protect the paint. You can apply as a spray or using a brush, depending on your preference.

Is there anything more fun than a pajama party?

Unicorn Sleep Mask

Popcorn, cookies, ice cream, and sleeping on the floor with all your friends can be one of the most fun experiences of your childhood.

This fun do-it-yourself project is the perfect craft to spend the afternoon making with friends before the pajama party starts. Everyone can make their own sleeping unicorn mask to cover their eyes when it's time for bed. It is an easy craft that can be done in less than two hours.

Supplies:

- Felt (colors: white, fuchsia, pink, light pink, black, purple, and green)
- Golden fabric
- Paper
- Scissors
- White elastic band
- Liquid silicone glue
- Masking tape

Figure 1

Instructions:

Trace the largest part of the template in Figure 1 in the center of a sheet of paper. Make note that this is only half of the mask.

Fold the paper along the straight line of the drawing and proceed to cut the outline with the scissors. By doing this, when you unfold the paper, you will have the complete and symmetrical template.

Trace and cut out the rest of the pieces from the template so you have all the pieces ready to move on to the next step.

May you have sweet dreams, adorable unicorns!

Stick each piece with masking tape onto its corresponding felt color. Then trim each piece one time, except for the white mask, which you must cut twice. Rather than felt, use shiny golden cloth for the horn.

Next, measure the back of your head from one ear to the other and cut a piece of elastic band that is ¾ inch smaller than that measurement. Glue it to one of the white mask pieces with liquid silicone glue. Reference the following image for placement.

Tip: Silicone takes more than thirty minutes to dry, so I advise, while drying, to clip the tape and felt with a clothespin to hold it in place.

I think this is going great, but there's something missing . . . who forgot to make popcorn? It's totally necessary to finish this craft! 😜

Meanwhile, stick the rest of the pieces on the other white felt in the following order: first stick the golden horn, next the fuchsia bangs, then the green leaves. On the leaves, stick the large piece of the flower, then paste the smaller piece of the flower, and on top, the yellow circle for the flower's center. Following will be the pink pieces of the ears and then, finally, the eyes.

Finally, glue both white pieces together using liquid silicone. Please note that you must leave the ends of the elastic band between them. Now, let it dry at least forty minutes. Before using it, it must be completely dry.

May you have sweet dreams, adorable unicorns!

Create fluffy slime with this homemade recipe!

Unicorn Fluffy Slime

Making homemade slime reminds me of my childhood. There was a time when I wanted to be a scientist and I made my own experiments by mixing kitchen ingredients with toothpaste and hand soap. I thought I would be able to invent something great, but instead the result was a horrible paste.

Luckily, I have now learned a slime recipe that does work. It can be made with simple household ingredients. I'll also show you how to make a unicorn version. Making slime is super easy and it won't take very long. It's also a relaxing craft, so you won't want to stop. I'm sure you'll spend hours playing with this fluffy slime.

Supplies:

- Bowl (large)
- White school glue
- Acrylic paints
- Spoon (to mix)
- Baking soda
- Shaving cream
- Saline solution for contact lenses

Instructions:

Okay, this is a lot like a cooking recipe (but it's not edible, so don't put it in your mouth)! Prepare to get a little dirty. Wash your hands before starting and wear older clothes so it doesn't matter if they get stained.

In a large bowl, add 4 1/5 fluid ounces of white school glue with half a teaspoon of whichever color acrylic paint you like most. Mix until the glue has absorbed the paint color.

Now, add half a teaspoon of baking soda and mix again to incorporate it.

Then add shaving cream (about one cup) and mix again. This will make the slime fluffy and pleasant to the touch because the foam causes the glue to fill with air bubbles.

Now is the time to turn all this into slime, and the ingredient that will make this possible is saline solution for contact lenses. Add several drops and mix in. You will see that it becomes thick and is hard to remove, but you should keep stirring. Continue adding drops of saline solution until the slime stops sticking to the walls of the bowl.

When you're at this point, you can pick it up with your hands and start playing.

To create unicorn slime, make this recipe using rainbow colors. You can take pieces of each color and combine them to make funny unicorn poops.

Relax by playing with this fluffy unicorn slime. When you finish playing, store it in a container with a lid so it doesn't dry out and you can play with it again another day. However, it's more fun to make the recipe every time!

Unicorn Story Stones

Once upon a time, brothers were bored on a road trip with their parents.

To entertain themselves, they invented games. For example: one game they thought up was to count all the red cars that they saw, or they sang songs from school. However, even those games got boring after a while.

One day while walking along the beach, they found smooth and flat stones, and they thought of creating a new game to make their car trips more fun.

This craft is easy. Basically, it's going to take the time you need to paint your stones; the more stones you paint, the more time it will take, but your story will ultimately be much longer and more fun.

Supplies:

- Flat and smooth stones (to make painting easier)
- Cloth bag
- Acrylic paints
- Pencil
- Brush
- Black permanent marker

Instructions:

Try to find stones that have a smooth surface and are no bigger than the palm of your hand. You can obtain them from beach areas or on the banks of rivers. Erosion from the water causes the stones to become rounded and smooth.

I just gave you the perfect excuse to persuade your family to take a walk on the beach or along the river. Tell them you need stones for a project. You will surely have a great time looking for them!

This project requires you to paint stones with different characters, places, and objects with which you can form a story. You know I love unicorns, princess stories, castles, and magic, so I'll incorporate these ideas into my bag of stones. First, draw on the stone with a pencil your character, place, or thing. I started by drawing a unicorn.

Now, fill your drawing with white paint. This will make the colors you add at a later stage look much more vivid. Before continuing, you should let the white paint dry. Do this step on several stones at once so that they can all dry simultaneously and decrease your wait time.

After a few minutes, once the stones are completely dry, you are ready for the next step. On top of the white paint, redraw with pencil the same design you did at the beginning, including all the details.

Then add color to your drawing with acrylic paints. Use a fine-tipped brush for more precise strokes, since the drawings will likely have some small, intricate details.

Wait a few minutes for the paint to dry. Then use a black permanent marker to outline the entire drawing. This includes the smaller details, not just the perimeter.

Get a cloth bag that is big enough to fit all the stones in it. And why not make it prettier? With a pencil, trace a phrase relating to the game. It can be simply "Story Stones," "Unicorn Stories," or something a little more detailed, i.e. "Once upon a time . . ."

Now fill in the phrase with black paint; it will give a more sophisticated touch. Then let it dry completely.

Reference all the drawings I have made. With these rocks, you could tell many exciting stories. They include everything you'd want in a magical story: a castle, a princess, a spell book, a magical unicorn potion, a frog, a carriage, a magic wand . . . among many more drawings with which you could form exciting stories.

Next, I will explain the rules of the game. If you want, you can write them on paper and insert them into the bag so that all participants can read them.

Yeah, but . . . how do you play?

Game rules:

1. Put all the stones in the bag.
2. Give it a good shake.
3. Pick your own way to start your story. I like to use, "Once upon a time . . ."
4. Once you start your story, pull out a stone from the bag and put it on the table.
5. Incorporate the drawing from the stone into your story; it should have coherent meaning.
6. Take turns! Pass the bag to the next player. Now they must choose another stone and continue your story with the drawing they pick.
7. Continue until the bag is empty or until the player who started the story says, "The End"

Surely a super fun and possibly crazy story will be formed!

Is it a cake? Looks like it, but it's not!

Unicorn Cake Storage Box

When I was a child, my mom spent the day yelling "Isa, clean your room!" I have never been very organized, but now I know why. It's because I didn't have a box as precious as this to organize all my treasures and trinkets.

In the following instructions, I will show you how to decorate a simple cardboard box so that it looks like a unicorn cake. If it was up to me, everything would look like candy and sweets!

Set aside an entire afternoon to make this box. The difficulty is medium because you must take specific measurements of your box so that everything is perfect, but I am sure you will make a great cake!

Supplies:

- Round cardboard box
- Foam paper (colors: white, pink, blue, yellow, purple, fuchsia, black, pink glitter, and blue glitter)
- Gold glitter
- Liquid silicone glue
- White glue
- Double-sided adhesive tape
- Bond paper
- Yellow Model Magic
- Gold acrylic paint
- Skewer
- Pink blush
- Brush
- Pencil
- Scissors

Instructions:

Try to get a round and tall cardboard box, my box is approximately 8 inches high and 7 inches in diameter.

First, mark with a pencil the place where the lid of the box ends. It is important not to cross into this area so that the box opens and closes without problems.

Measure the distance from this mark to the base of the box. You must also measure the circumference of the box and with these measurements cut a piece of white foam paper. This will be the body of the cake. Glue it onto the box with liquid silicone glue. You must repeat the same procedure with the lid.

In the next step, we will make the unicorn's mane. To stick with the cake theme, we should imitate the shapes that a pastry bag makes with buttercream. Therefore, draw the two forms shown in "Figure 1" on paper. By doing so, we will form two different sizes.

Figure 1

Cut out these shapes and use them as a template to trace on foam paper. You will need many of these shapes in various colors. I think the ideal colors for unicorn hair are blue, purple, pink, yellow, and fuchsia, but feel free to use whatever colors you like. The box that I made has approximately fifty "buttercream flowers," so this kept me entertained for quite a while!

This box already looks like a fondant cake. What follows next is a cinch!

With the help of the scissors, cut out all the shapes and place a piece of double-sided adhesive tape right in the center.

To simulate the buttercream flower shape, you should stick each tip of the petals in the center of the flower. Reference the following image for visual aid.

Real unicorn cakes have a horn made with fondant. However, in this project, we will use Model Magic to make it. This modeling compound is very similar to fondant, so no one will notice the difference. Take a good amount of dough and stretch it into a very long strand. Make it so it has one pointed end and one thicker end. Roll it into a spiral to form the horn. Once you have formed the horn, stick a thin wooden stick through the bottom (wider side). This will help the horn maintain its shape while it dries. I used a skewer. I'm sure you can find one in your kitchen, but if not, they sell them in most grocery stores or online.

To give a chic touch to our cake, add gold acrylic paint and glitter. First, paint the horn with the acrylic paint and let it dry. Then, apply a layer of white glue and sprinkle it with gold glitter. Finally, let it dry completely.

Have you ever noticed that the unicorn ears are shaped like upside-down hearts? I'm sure now you think I've lost my mind, but observe . . .

In Figure 2, you can see two hearts—one that's larger and one that's smaller. Take a piece of paper and a pencil, draw the outlines, and cut them out.

Figure 2

Using this as a template, you must create two larger hearts using white foam paper and two smaller hearts using pink glitter foam paper. Apply liquid silicone glue to stick the small heart in the center of the big heart as shown. Next, apply a small amount of glue on the bottom of the ear (wide area of the heart) and glue it together to form a three-dimensional unicorn ear.

Now, it's time to assemble all the parts and form the cake. Use liquid silicone glue to stick the horn to the lid. Place the horn closer to the front, rather than exactly in the center of the lid. The ears should be placed on each side of the horn.

It's time to paste the buttercream flowers. Arrange them as if they made up the mane of a unicorn. Place some on the front of the unicorn to form its bangs and then add more to the area behind the horn. You can also place a few on the side to form a "buttercream flower" waterfall.

Do not forget to put eyes on this unicorn. Draw "Figure 3" and cut two equal templates (one for the right eye and one for the left), and then use the template to trace and cut two pieces of black foam paper in the shape of closed eyes, then stick them on the cake.

To complete the project, decorate the base of the cake using the blue and pink glitter foam paper to form two very long strips. Make one of them ¾ inch wide and the other ⅖ inch wide. Glue them with liquid silicone around the lower part of the cake.

As a final touch, add rosy cheeks. This gives a great kawaii look. You can use pink blush to do so.

Figure 3

Oh, no! I suddenly feel like eating a piece of cake!

Amazing! I never thought that a cardboard box could be transformed into something so beautiful! I think we deserve a treat. What about some cake?

I admit that sometimes I would love to be a unicorn.

Unicorn Headband

#IamAUnicorn #UnicornParty #UnicornSelfie #UnicornHair
#UnicornDance #IsasUnicornCrafts

Create your own unicorn headband, and you won't stop taking selfies! This hair accessory is ideal for a unicorn party or to complete a costume. Personally, I would use it for every occasion because I love it! Organize an afternoon of magical crafts with your friends; it will be fun to form a whole unicorn team!

This craft is going to take approximately sixty minutes, and its difficulty is medium because we are going to sew. However, if this part is difficult for you, you can always replace the seam with a line of glue, so there are no excuses. Let's get started!

Supplies:

- Headband (I chose one with a golden cord, but any type will work.)
- Pink glitter foam paper
- White felt
- Shiny golden fabric
- Fiber filling
- Artificial flowers
- Slim gold cord
- Thread and needle
- Scissors
- Pencil and paper

Instructions:

Take a paper and pencil and draw each of the shapes from Figure 1, then cut them out.

Figure 1

Take the golden fabric and the cone-shaped template and cut this shape out of the fabric. You can mark it with a pencil or with masking tape.

Bend the cone in half and thread the needle to sew the straight edge closed. Start sewing just under the tip of the cone.

If sewing is difficult for you, you can replace the seam with a thin line of glue, but let it dry before continuing. Remember that the shiny gold part should be on the inside. Do not sew or glue the mouth of the cone. Leave this open. Now we must flip the cone, but just before flipping it completely, take the slim golden cord and insert it through the hole we have left at the tip.

Tie a knot in the cord and pull it from the tip so the knot is tight inside the cone.

Using the cone as a template, let's draw a felt circle that is the size of the base, then cut out this circle.

In this step, we will stuff the cone with fiber filling. It only requires a little fiber filling, so you can take it from a cushion that you find in your house or use cotton balls.

Apply glue to the inner contour of the cone. Do not add too much, we don't want it to overflow and make a mess.

This is going to be awesome!

Stick the felt circle to close the cone. Try to keep the circle inside the cone for better results. Let the glue dry for approximately five minutes.

Apply a small drop of glue on the tip of the horn and glue the cord so it does not move. Wait for the glue to dry before continuing. Then roll the cord in a spiral down to the base.

Glue the cord at the base and cut the surplus.

Great! We have completed the most difficult part of the project. From now on, everything is simple. To celebrate, we are going to dance "the dance of the unicorn!" You can invent your own steps.

Cut out another felt circle. We will glue the headband between the horn and the felt circle with liquid silicone glue. Make sure that the horn is centered!

Next, use the smallest template to cut out the inner ear shape two times in the foam paper.

The medium-sized template will be used to create the outer part of the ears. Using the template, trace the outline twice on white felt and cut out.

The last step is to add artificial flowers to decorate our headband. Use as many as you want and combine the colors to your preference. Let the glue dry before using the headband.

Place the headband in the center of the felt ear, apply glue inside, and fold it in half so it stays stuck. Then stick the small pink piece in the center of the ear. Repeat this step on the opposite side of the horn for the other ear.

Well done! Our unicorn headband is ready! How about a funny photo? Say "Selfiiiiee!"

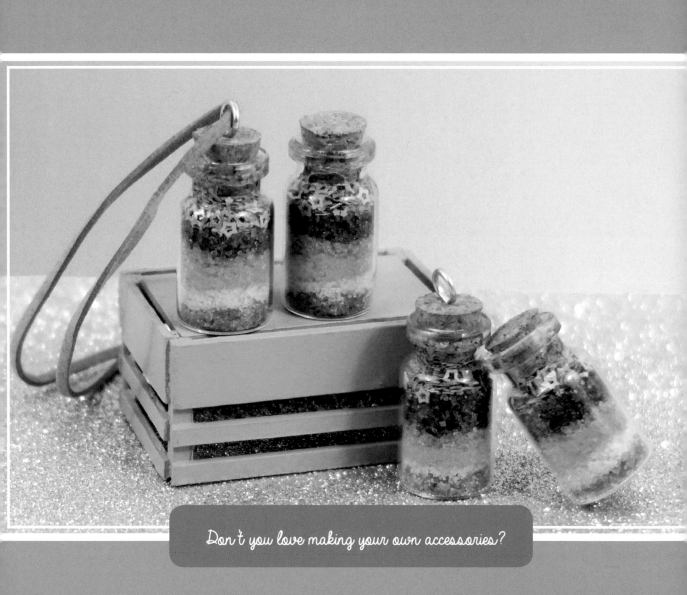

Don't you love making your own accessories?

Unicorn Magic Charm

#UnicornGift #UnicornBFF #UnicornNecklace
#UnicornMagic #IsasUnicornCrafts

Imagine having your own pendant that contains the magic of unicorns. You can also make several of these beautiful charms to give to your best friends!

Seriously, this craft is super easy and super fast. You likely won't spend more than twenty minutes working on it. No, you will not have to go to look for a unicorn to capture its magic; you will only need salt and a few other things.

Supplies:

- Coarse salt
- Paper
- Colored chalk
- Star-shaped glitter (a few colors)
- Liquid silicone
- Small glass bottles with cork stoppers
- Small screw eyes
- Cord necklace

Instructions:

Put a small amount of salt on a piece of paper.

Take your chalk and rub it over the salt. Soon you will see the salt change colors to match the chalk!

Repeat this step with five different colors. If you want, you can use the same colors as I did. I tried to make it similar to the colors of the rainbow.

Using the paper as a funnel, pour a small amount of each colored salt into your small glass bottle. Ideally, you want to form layers of the same size for each color. Do not fill it completely, leave some space above to fill it with colored stars.

If you prefer, you can stop here and you will have a beautiful magic charm, or you can turn it into a necklace! For this, you need a small screw eye. Screw it in the center of the cork and then run a cord or chain through it to hang it from your neck.

It is important that the unicorn magic does not escape, so add a little liquid silicone glue and then push in the cork stopper.

I can already feel the magic of unicorns flowing. Now I am ready accomplish anything! 😉

CONCLUSION

I hope you have enjoyed your trip through the pages of this book. For me, it has been a pleasure to create these twenty-seven unicorn projects for you. I put a lot of love into each of them.

Remember that "life looks more beautiful from the back of a unicorn." This is just a saying to remind you that your imagination has no limits and that you can create anything you set your mind to.

Never lose your creative spirit and put passion into everything you do in your life.

Thank you for immersing yourself in these pages and do not forget: Be a unicorn!

With love, Isa ♡

About the Author

Isabel Urbina Gallego (Madrid, Spain)

Isabel has always been a creative person. When she was a child, she spent her leisure time teaching herself how to do handicrafts. In 2014, she decided to turn this hobby into something professional. That's when she created her first YouTube channel called El Mundo de Isa, where, weekly, she teaches her viewers to make beautiful crafts from scratch in Spanish, her native tongue. She teaches crafts for both children and adults.

Her community of fans soon spread like a wildfire and that is why she wanted to expand borders by creating a new channel on YouTube called Isa's World, where she explains her creations in English.

In 2016, the Vlogger Prize for best crafts channel of the year was awarded to El Mundo de Isa. Since then, Isabel has not stopped doing all kinds of crafts because it is her passion.

She loves to spend time with her family, but some of her best moments are in the company of her two dogs Arish and Noah, and with her sentimental and professional partner Víctor Vic.

Youtube: www.youtube.com/Mundodeisa and www.youtube.com/c/IsasWorld

Facebook: www.facebook.com/isalunahe

Instagram: www.instagram.com/isalunahe

Twitter: www.twitter.com/isalunahe

blog: www.elmundodeisa.com

Acknowledgments

This is my first book, and it is the first time that I have embarked on a project like this. I have put all my love into every page and project. I never thought I would have my own book, so this is a dream come true.

I feel so grateful that it is difficult to express this feeling with words. Thanks to all my followers because they are the main component that makes this possible. *Isa's World* and *El Mundo de Isa* make me feel so loved with every "like" and with every comment, always with beautiful phrases that motivate me to continue creating for you. I love each and every one of you. Thanks for being there every time I upload a new video.

To my boyfriend, Victor—my partner, my traveling companion, my love—thank you for believing in all my crazy ideas and for helping me make them become a reality. Thanks for your help and unconditional support both in life and with my job. We make a great team, working hand in hand, and we will always achieve whatever we set out to do. Thanks for taking care of me and for accompanying me. I love you.

To my editor, Jason Schneider, for giving me this opportunity. Without knowing me, you believed in me. Thank you for your trust and for your patience.

To my parents, Teresa and Santiago, first for giving me life and then for always trusting me. You like everything I do, all my ideas seem good, and you never question my decisions. By doing so, you make me feel important. I love you with all my heart. Thank you!

To my sisters—Lorena, Azucena, and Teresa—for valuing my ideas, my opinions, and my work. I know that I can always count on you to make me feel protected like a baby kangaroo tucked in its mother's pouch. Knowing that you are there, I am not afraid of almost anything. Thank you for being my life teachers.

To the rest of my family, to my *Tita* Isabel, to all my nephews, and to my brothers-in-law, because you are there to share my posts, to give them a like, and to contribute your feedback. Thanks for all your support, you are great!

To my other family, that of my boyfriend, Mercedes, Manuel, and Angel, thank you for "adopting" me and treating me as one more of your own, for integrating me into the family from the first day, and for your help whenever we have needed it. I feel that I have two moms, two dads, and one brother.

Thanks to my two guardian angels, my hairy puppies Arish and Noah, who are inseparable companions that make me happy every morning and fill my heart with joy.

To my friends and colleagues, Youtubers from the WhatsApp group, thank you for your advice and for sharing your experiences. You have been a great help.

And thanks to those of you who are reading this book. Without you, this would not make sense.